A-Z

of

CLASSICAL
MUSIC

Music Sales America

EXCLUSIVELY DISTRIBUTED BY

HAL•LEONARD®
CORPORATION
7777 W. BLUEMOUND RD. P.O. BOX 13819 MILWAUKEE, WI 53213

Published by
Amsco Publications,
257 Park Avenue South, New York, NY 10010 USA.

Music Sales Limited,
Distribution Centre, Newmarket Road, Bury St Edmunds,
Suffolk, IP33 3YB, UK.

Music Sales Pty Limited,
20 Resolution Drive,
Caringbah, NSW 2229, Australia.

Order No. AM994631
ISBN 978-0-8256-3680-6

Compiled and edited by Jessica Williams.
Cover Design by Ruth Keating.

Printed in the United States of America.

Your Guarantee of Quality

As publishers, we strive to produce every book
to the highest commercial standards.

This book has been carefully designed to minimize awkward page
turns and to make playing from it a real pleasure. Particular care has
been given to specifying acid-free, neutral-sized paper made from pulps
which have not been elemental chlorine bleached.

This pulp is from farmed sustainable forests and
was produced with special regard for the environment.

Throughout, the printing and binding have been planned to ensure
a sturdy, attractive publication which should give years of enjoyment.

If your copy fails to meet our high standards, please inform us
and we will gladly replace it.

www.musicsales.com

Ave Maria

Composed by Franz Schubert

Adagio

Air on the G String

Composed by Johann Sebastian Bach

The Arrival of the Queen of Sheba

Composed by George Frideric Handel

Allegro

Barcarolle

(from *The Tales of Hoffmann*)

Composed by Jacques Offenbach

Allegretto moderato

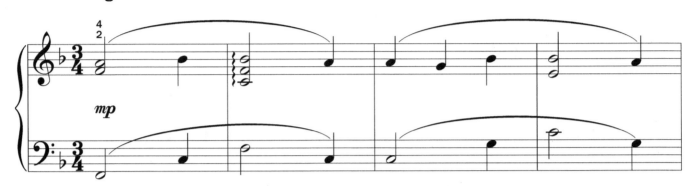

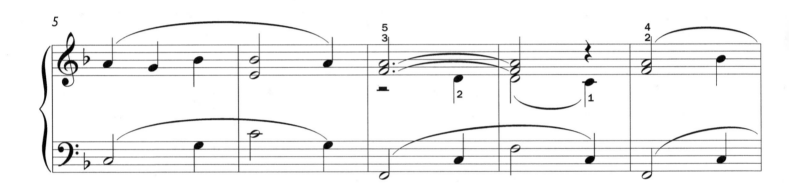

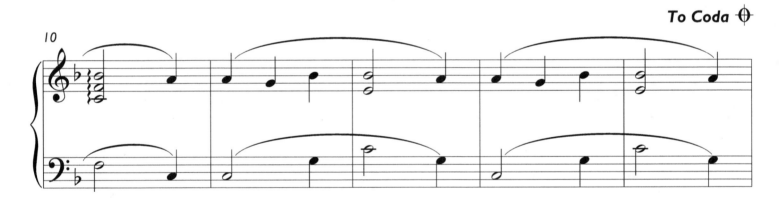

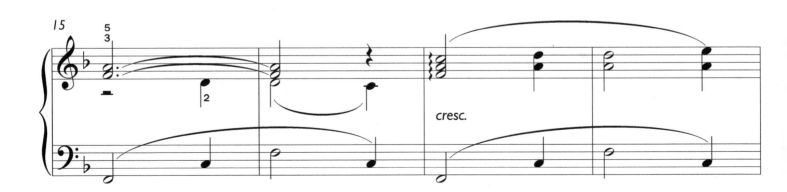

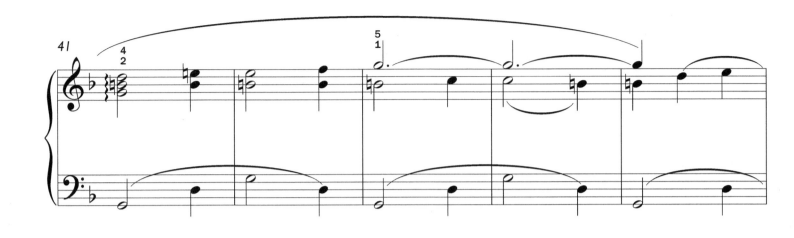

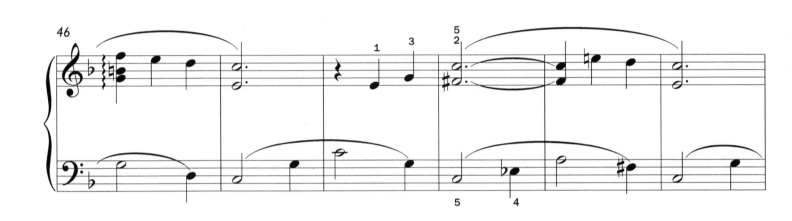

D.C. al Coda

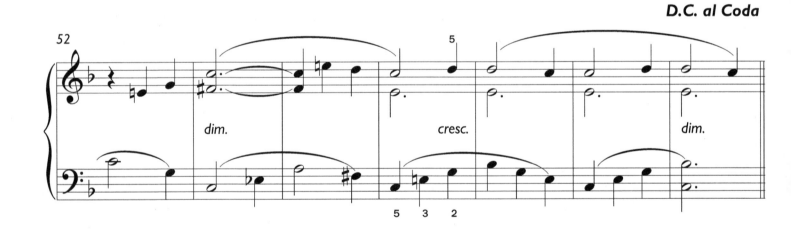

⊕ **Coda**

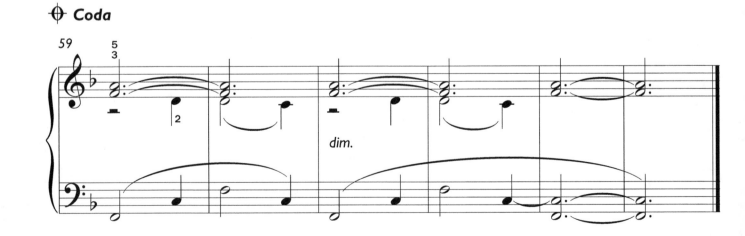

The Birdcatcher's Song

(from *The Magic Flute*)

Composed by Wolfgang Amadeus Mozart

*The small notes indicate the original version which can be played instead of the simplified version if preferred.

Brandenburg Concerto No.6
(2nd Movement)

Composed by Johann Sebastian Bach

Adagio, ma non tanto

The Can Can

(from *Orpheus in the Underworld*)

Composed by Jacques Offenbach

Canon in D

Composed by Johann Pachelbel

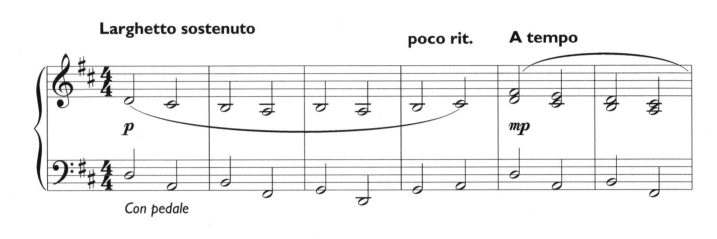

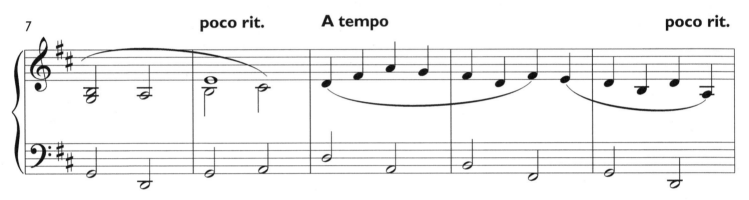

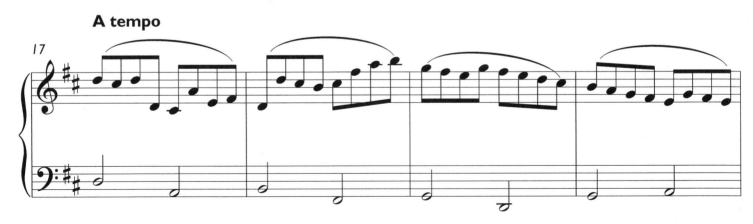

Christmas Concerto
(3rd Movement: "Pastorale")

Composed by Arcangelo Corelli

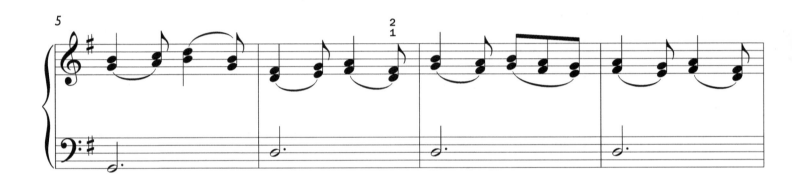

Clair de Lune

Composed by Claude Debussy

Dance of the Blessed Spirits

(from *Orfeo ed Euridice*)

Composed by Christoph Willibald von Gluck

La Donna è Mobile

(from *Rigoletto*)

Composed by Giuseppe Verdi

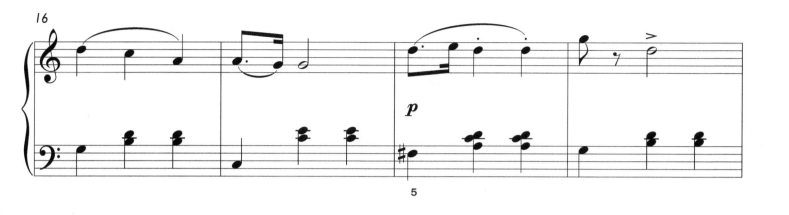

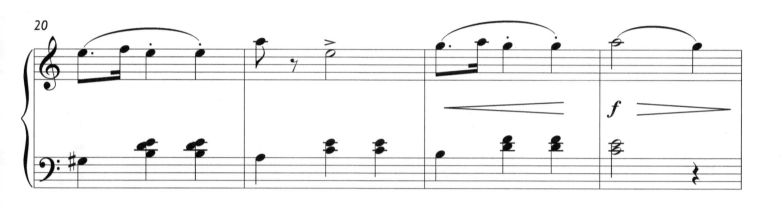

Fine

D.C. al Fine

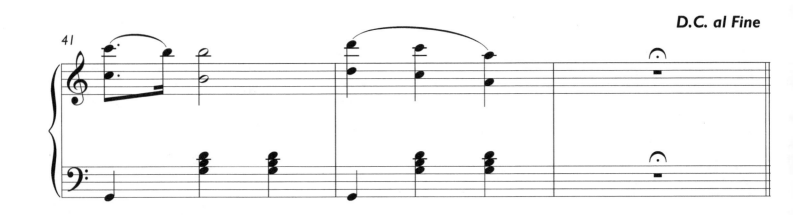

German Dance

("The Sleigh Ride")

Composed by Wolfgang Amadeus Mozart

Eine kleine Nachtmusik
(1st Movement)

Composed by Wolfgang Amadeus Mozart

Enigma Variations
(Theme)

Composed by Sir Edward Elgar

Andante

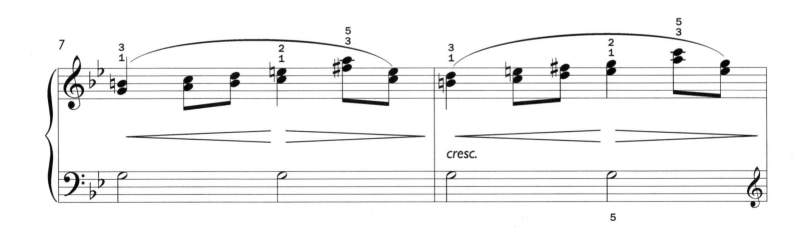

Etude No.3

Op.10

Composed by Frédéric Chopin

Flower Duet
(from *Lakmé*)

Composed by Leo Delibes

Andantino con moto

Für Elise

Composed by Ludwig van Beethoven

Andante con moto

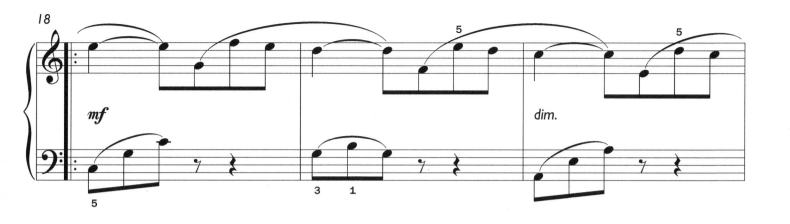

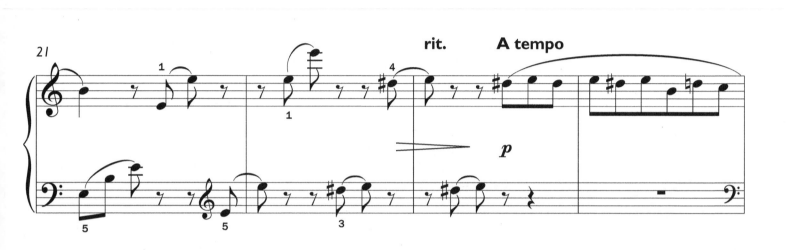

Gymnopédie No.1

Composed by Erik Satie

Adagio

Habañera

(from *Carmen*)

Composed by Georges Bizet
All Rights Reserved. International Copyright Secured.

Allegro quasi andantino

* ⌐♩♩♩¬ original rhythm
  └─3─┘

"Hallelujah" Chorus
(from *Messiah*)

Composed by George Frideric Handel

Allegro con spiritoso

Horn Concerto No.4
(3rd Movement)

Composed by Wolfgang Amadeus Mozart

D.S. al Coda

Coda

Imperial March

Composed by Sir Edward Elgar

allargando

rit.

Italian Concerto

Composed by Johann Sebastian Bach

Impromptu No.3

Composed by Franz Schubert

Jesu, Joy of Man's Desiring

Composed by Johann Sebastian Bach

"Jupiter" Symphony No.41
(3rd Movement)

Composed by Wolfgang Amadeus Mozart

"Land of Hope and Glory"
(*Pomp and Circumstance March* No.1)

Composed by Sir Edward Elgar

Largamente

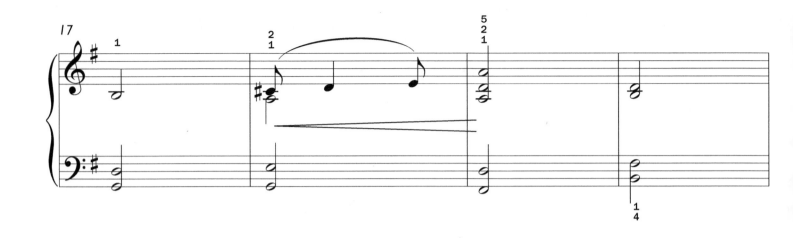

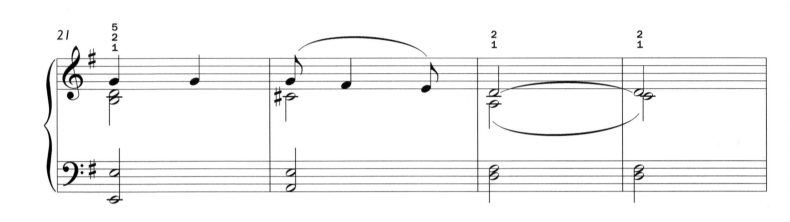

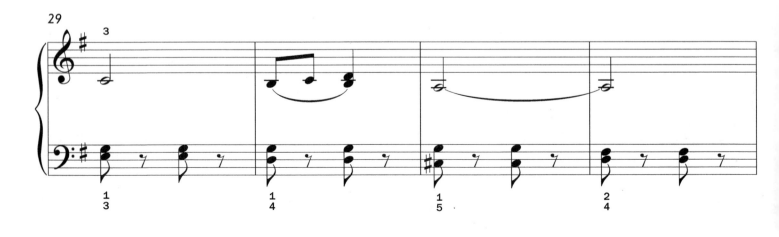

Kyrie Eleison

(from Mass No.12)

Composed by Wolfgang Amadeus Mozart

Largo

Composed by Arcangelo Corelli

Liebesträume

Composed by Franz Liszt

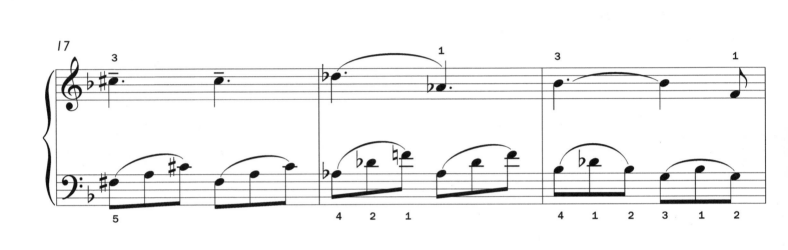

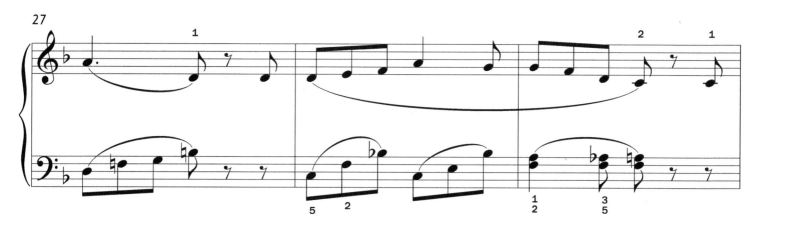

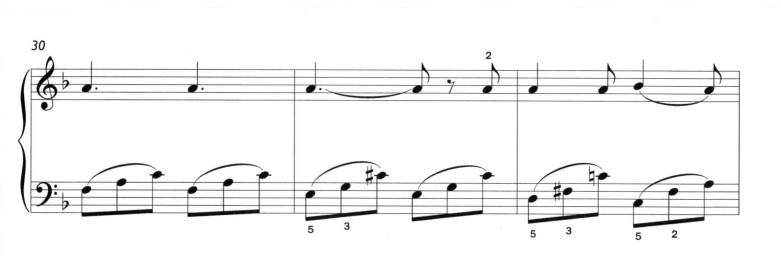

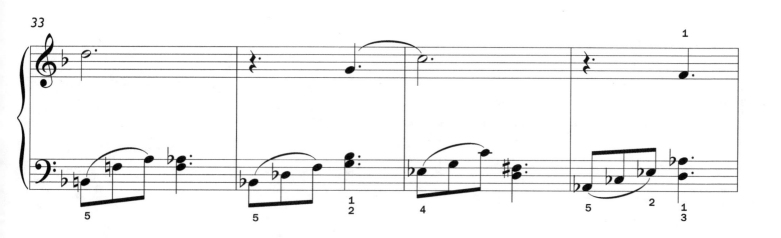

rit.

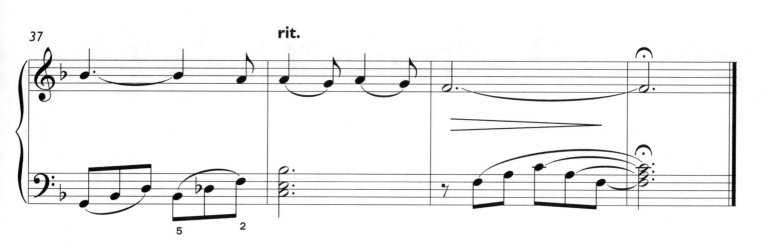

Little Prelude in C

Composed by Johann Sebastian Bach

Nocturne No.2
Op.9

Composed by Frédéric Chopin

Mazurka No.2

Op.67

Composed by Frédéric Chopin

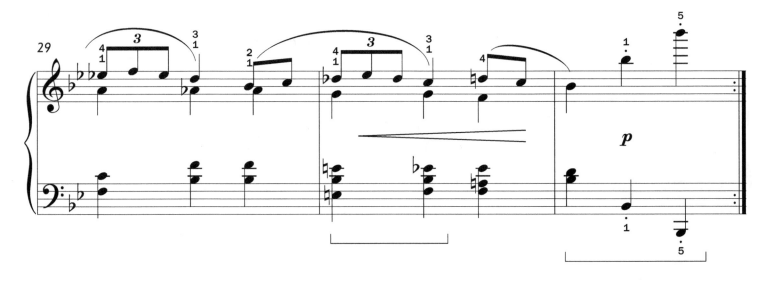

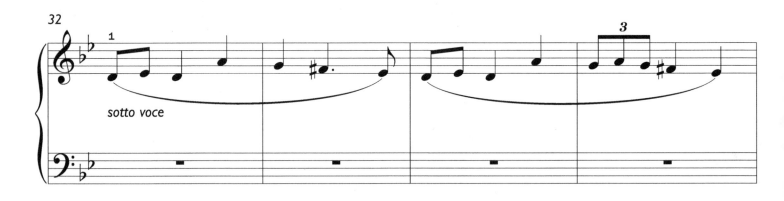

Minuet in G

Composed by Johann Sebastian Bach

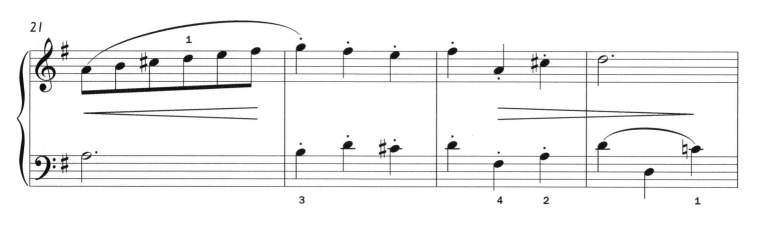

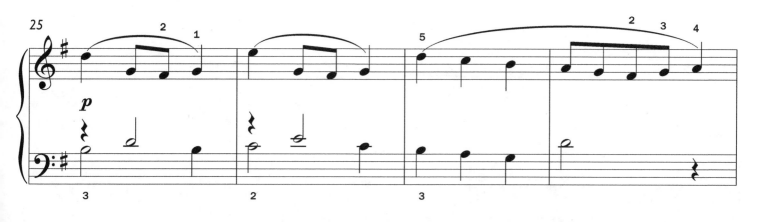

"Moonlight" Sonata

Op.27, No.2

Composed by Ludwig van Beethoven

Adagio sostenuto

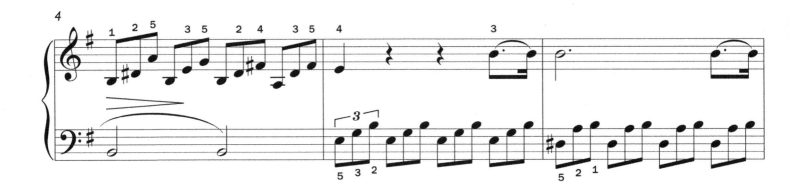

poco rit.   **A tempo**

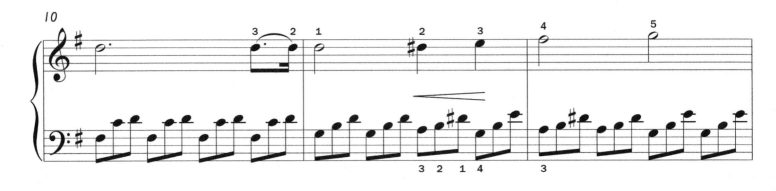

Nimrod
(from *Enigma Variations*)

Composed by Sir Edward Elgar

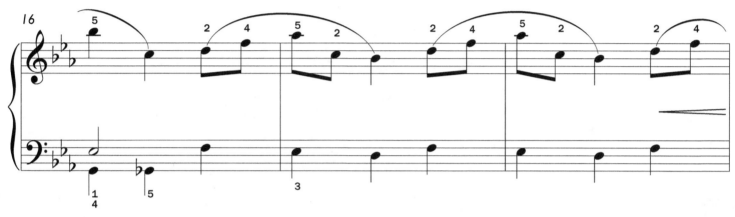

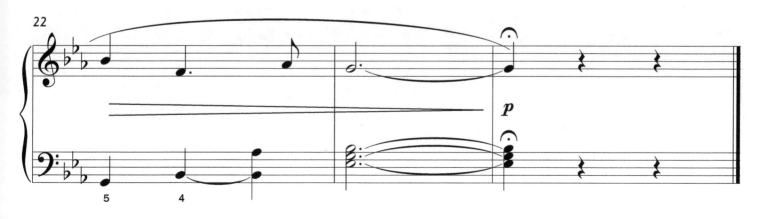

O, for the Wings of a Dove

Composed by Felix Mendelssohn

Ode to Joy
(from Symphony No.9 "Choral")

Composed by Ludwig van Beethoven

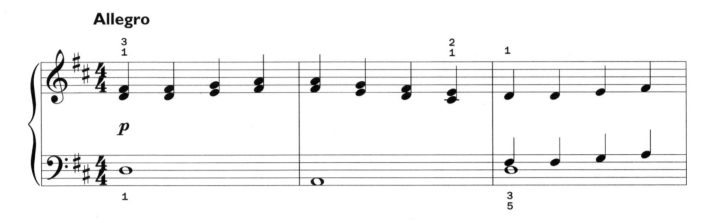

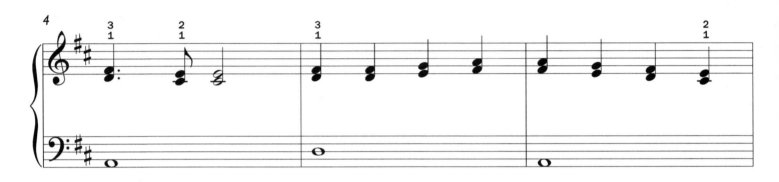

poco rit.

98

Panis Angelicus

Composed by César Franck

Pictures at an Exhibition
(Promenade)

Composed by Modest Mussorgsky

Allegro giusto, nel modo Russico, senza allegreza, ma poco sostenuto

Pie Jesu
(from Requiem Op.48)

Composed by Gabriel Fauré

String Quartet No.2
(3rd Movement Theme)

Composed by Alexander Borodin

Andante

"Raindrop" Prelude No.15
Op.28

Composed by Frédéric Chopin

The Ride of the Valkyries

(from *Die Walküre*)

Composed by Richard Wagner

The Swan

(from *The Carnival of the Animals*)

Composed by Camille Saint-Saëns

Andantino grazioso

Spring

(from *The Four Seasons*)

Composed by Antonio Vivaldi

"Scottish" Symphony No.3
(1st Movement)

Composed by Felix Mendelssohn

Andante con moto

Allegro un poco agitato

Tempo primo

D.S. al Fine

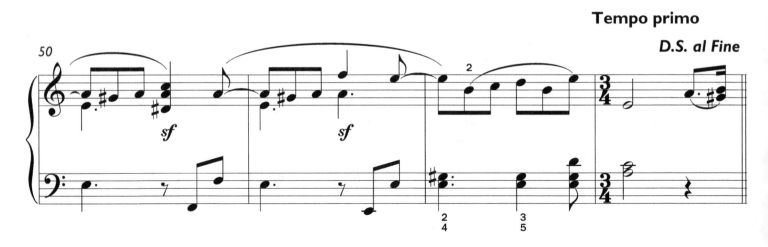

Symphony No.5
(4th Movement)

Composed by Gustav Mahler

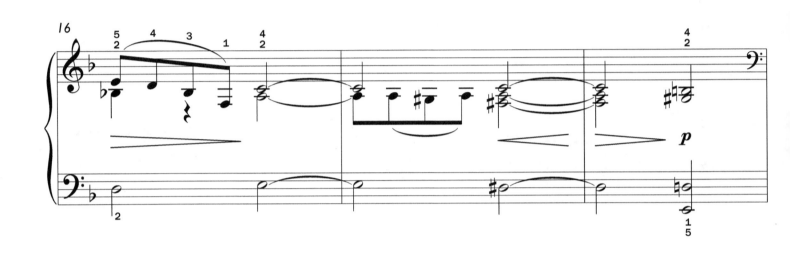

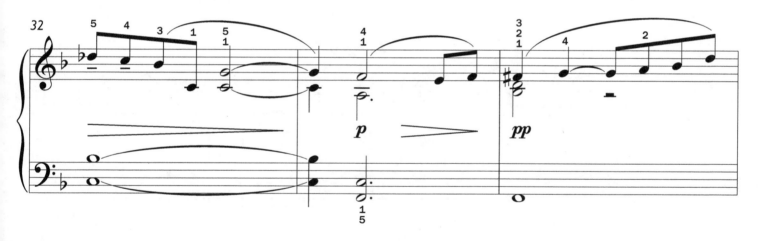

Toccata and Fugue in D Minor

Composed by Johann Sebastian Bach

Träumerei

Composed by Robert Schumann

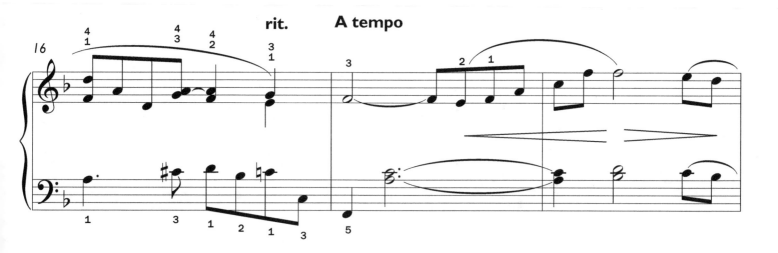

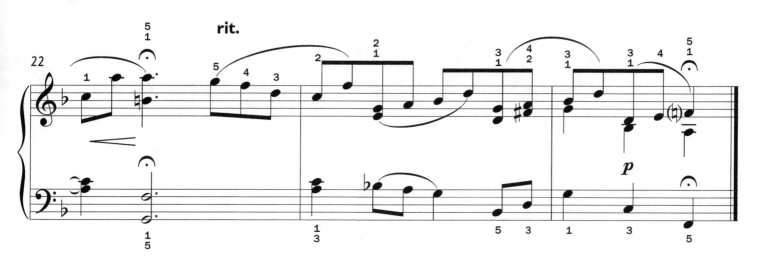

Trout Quintet
(4th Movement)

Composed by Franz Schubert

The Unfinished Symphony
(Theme)

Composed by Franz Schubert

Variations on "Ah, Vous Dirai-je, Maman"

Composed by Wolfgang Amadeus Mozart

Violin Concerto No.1
(2nd Movement)

Composed by Max Bruch

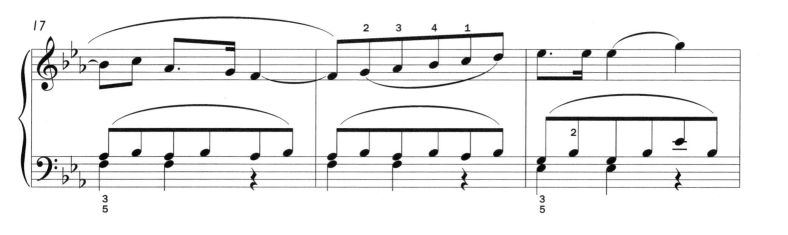

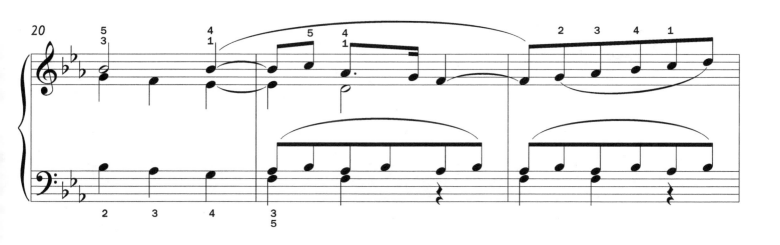

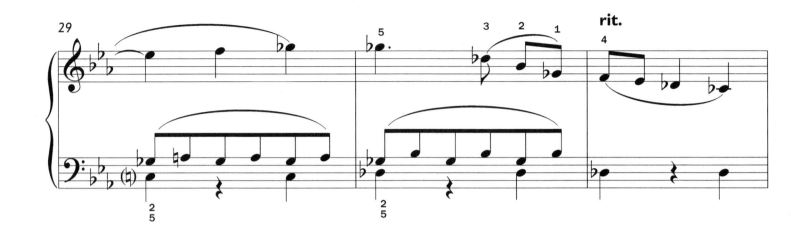

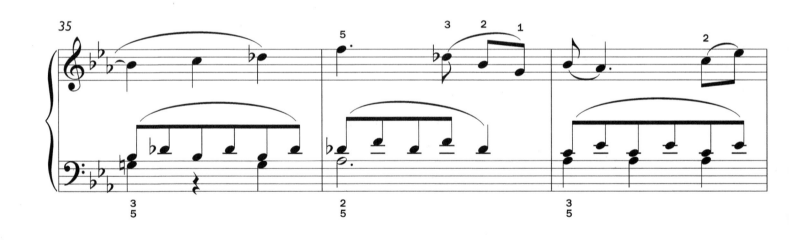

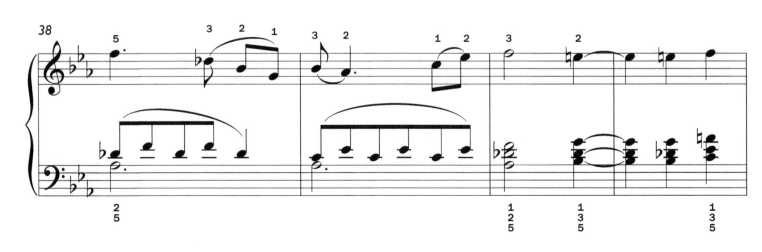

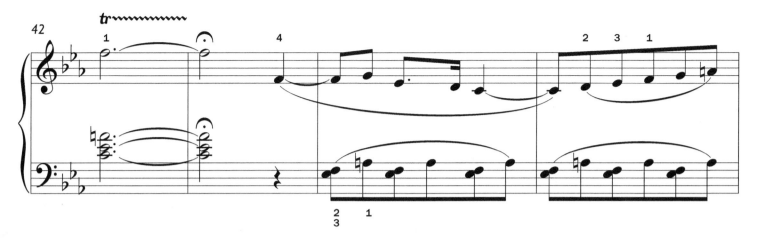

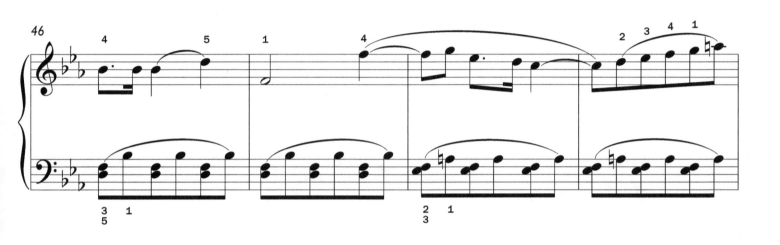

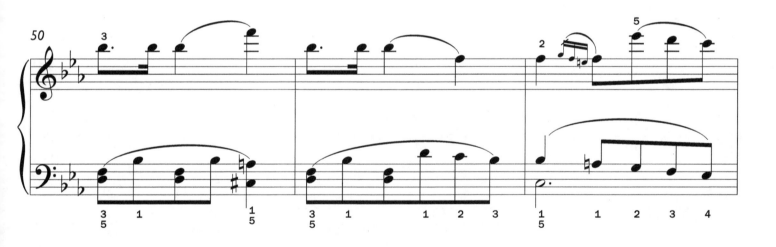

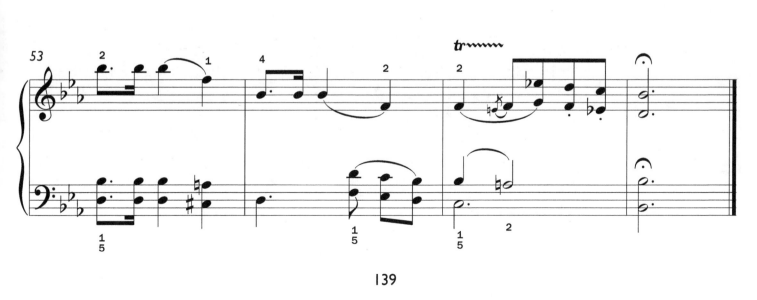

Waltz
(from *The Sleeping Beauty*)

Composed by Peter Ilyich Tchaikovsky

Allegro (Tempo di valse)

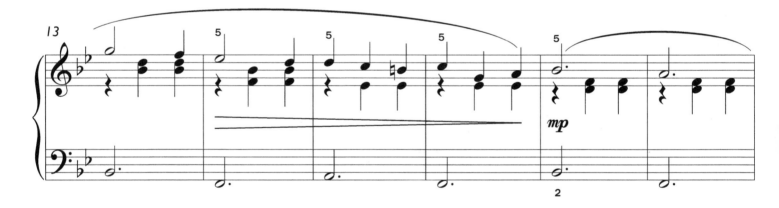

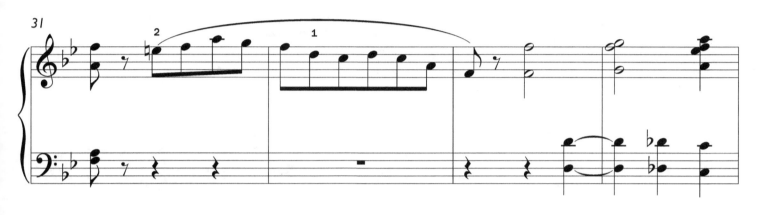

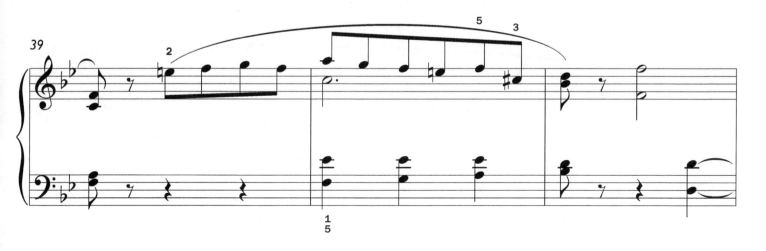

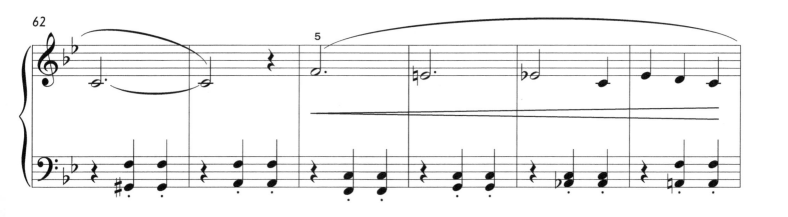

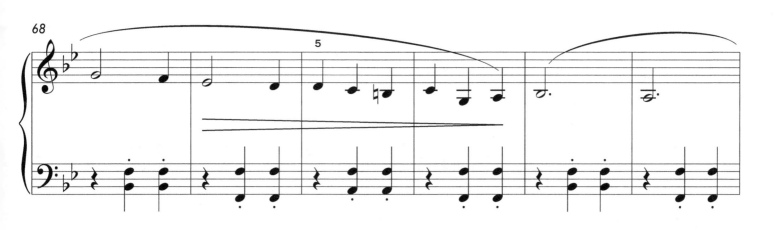

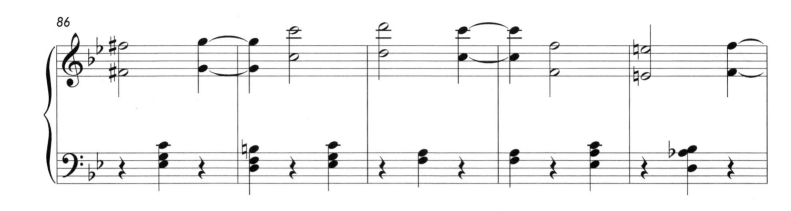

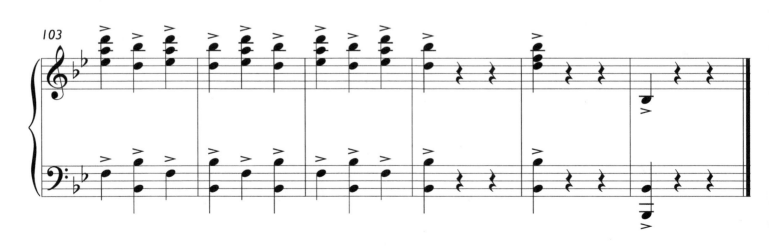

When I Am Laid in Earth

(from *Dido and Aeneas*)

Composed by Henry Purcell

William Tell Overture

(Theme)

Composed by Gioachino Rossini

Allegro vivace

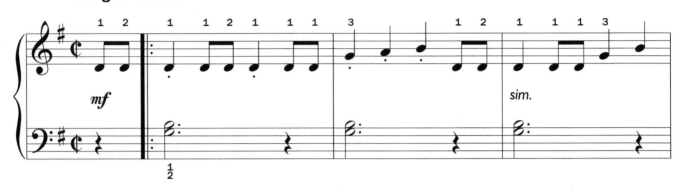

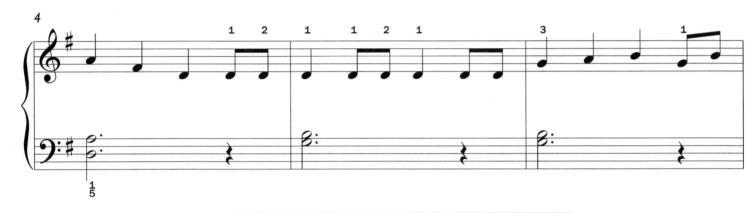

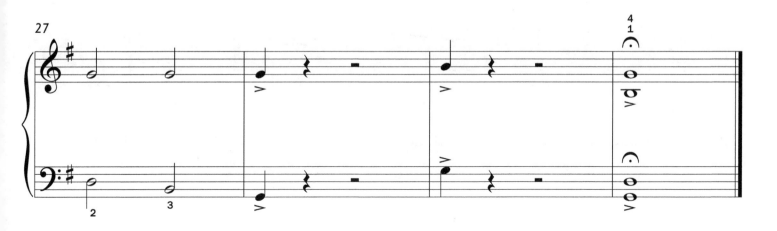

Winter
(from *The Four Seasons*)

Composed by Antonio Vivaldi

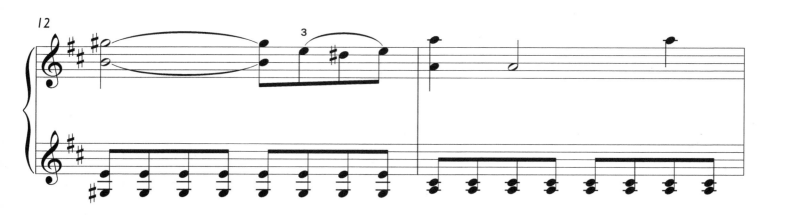

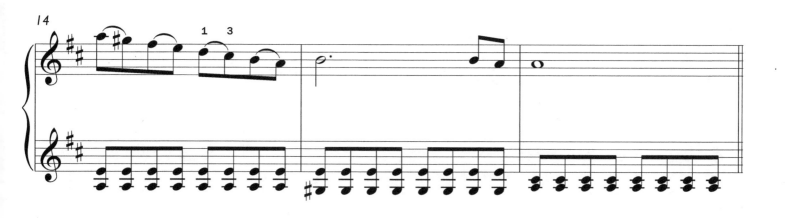

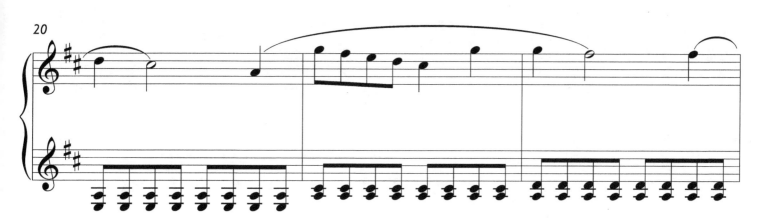

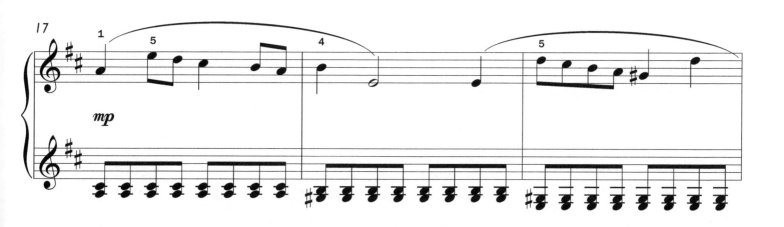

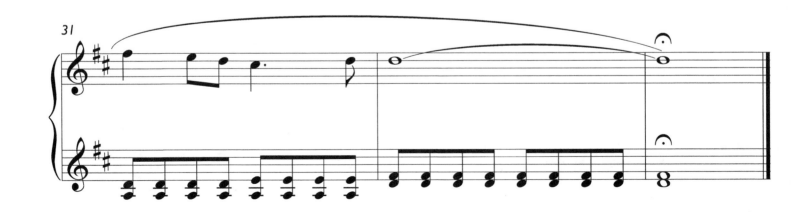

Xerxes
(Largo)

Composed by George Frideric Handel

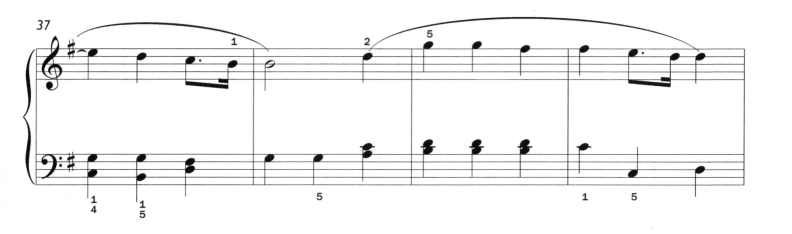

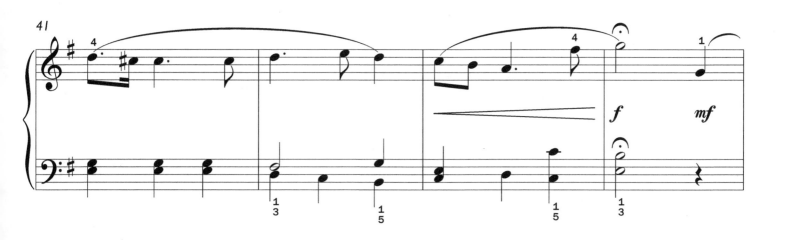

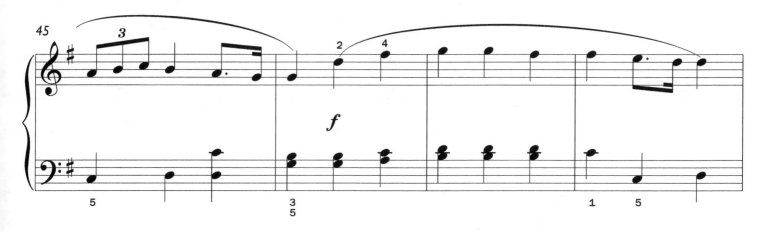

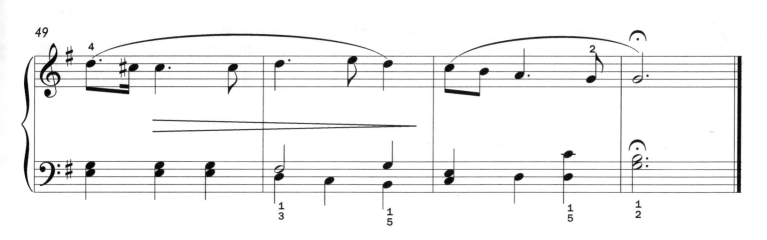

The Young Prince and the Princess

(from *Sheherazade*)

Composed by Nikolay Rimsky-Korsakov

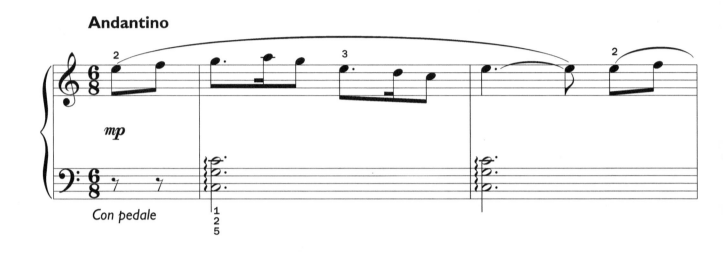

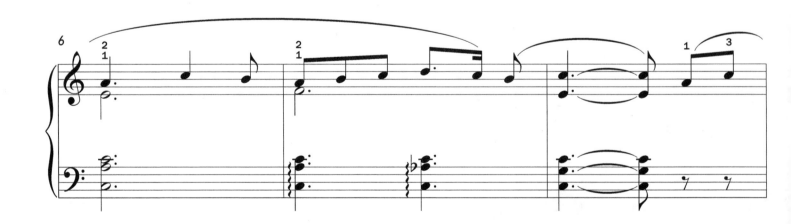

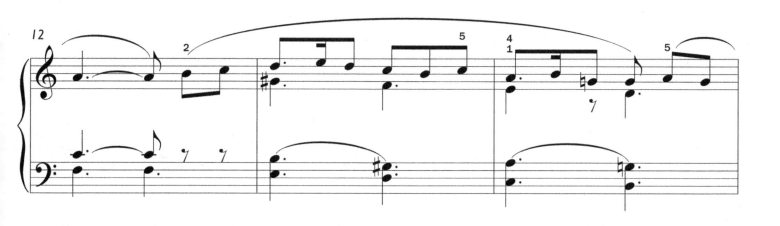

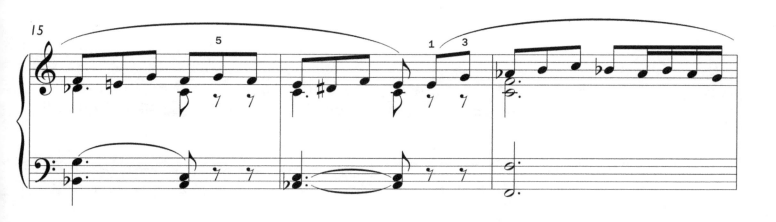

Zadok the Priest

Composed by George Frideric Handel

Andante maestro

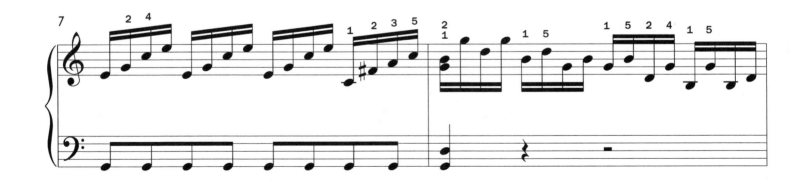

123456789